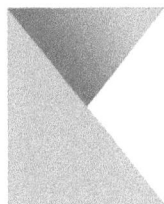

KEMPER
FOUNDATION

Insurance Basics

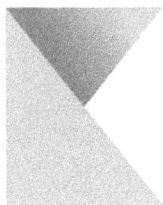

KEMPER
FOUNDATION

Insurance Basics

by

Mike Moyer and Jerry Fuller

Made possible through a grant from

The James S. Kemper Foundation

Published by the James S. Kemper Foundation
Chicago, IL
www.JSKemper.org

This book and online course are dedicated to the many bright students who are unfamiliar with the business world and have not yet decided on a career path. Our hope is that this information will help them understand how insurance companies function and be successful in their internships and first jobs.

FOREWORD

In 1942, James S. Kemper established an independent, private foundation. Today the Kemper Foundation continues to thrive as it gives back to the community through grants and scholarships and by developing future business leaders—with a special focus on the insurance industry.

As part of this effort, we sponsor a successful internship program designed to help undergraduate students develop skills and prepare for their careers.

With our roots in the insurance business, we believe this "Insurance Basics" book furthers our mission by providing practical advice to navigate an insurance industry career. To supplement this book, we offer a course at jskemper.org.

We encourage Kemper Scholars to learn all they can through this book, the online insurance course and their internships. We remain committed to developing the next generation of leaders in the insurance industry.

Sincerely,

Joseph P. Lacher, Jr.
President and Chief Executive Officer
Kemper Corporation

Chairman,
James S. Kemper Foundation Board of Trustees

CONTENTS

INTRODUCTION

In 2013 *Forbes* magazine ranked "actuary" as the top-rated job because it offers an enjoyable work environment and high salary. They projected a 27 percent growth in demand for actuaries by 2020. An actuary is just one of the many exciting and intellectually stimulating jobs in the insurance industry. Insurance is a critical component of any society because it allows people to protect what they have worked for.

People all over the world work hard to build the lives they want to live. They get married, start families, build businesses and acquire things—like houses and cars—that they think will add to their overall comfort and happiness.

In the process of building their lives they take on responsibilities and obligations both financially and personally. For instance, a person might take on financial responsibility by taking out a loan to buy a house, or she might take on personal obligations like having children or supporting a stay-at-home spouse. The more people take on, the more they have to lose.

Some of the risks they face are based on their own choices, but others are outside of their control. When people fear losing what they have built they will consider protecting it with insurance.

Insurance is the business of protecting people's businesses and lifestyles from events outside of their immediate control. It is a noble and important part of any successful economy and it can be an exciting place to build a career. Knowing that you are helping people protect what's important to them can be a very satisfying profession.

The purpose of this book is to familiarize you with the insurance industry, how it works, and how you can prepare yourself for your part in it.

If you're one of the literally millions of people who want to work in the industry, this book will help you get a leg up on the competition, and help you position yourself as a great job candidate for insurance companies.

Chapter One:

THE HISTORY OF INSURANCE

Some of the first examples of insurance occurred thousands of years ago when Chinese merchants divided their cargo across a number of different ships to reduce the risk of losing the entire cargo due to one event, that is, one storm that would sink one ship containing all of the cargo. Some of the ships would sink during storms, so some of the cargo would be lost, but the other ships would sail safely with the remaining cargo, so the merchant didn't suffer a total loss. Splitting up the shipment was more expensive than putting it on one boat, but the extra cost was well worth it to protect the entire investment.

Dividing up cargo across ships worked well if there were a lot of ships in the water, but there may not always have been a lot of options—especially thousands of years ago! So, merchants who borrowed money to finance their business operations would sometimes pay their lenders extra, if their lenders would agree to forgive the loan if the cargo was lost.

In Babylonia, King Hammurabi had the "Hammurabi Code" carved on an obelisk. The code provided, among other things, a sort of insurance that required creditors to forgive debt of those who fell victim to some personal catastrophe—such as disability, death or flooding—that made it impossible for them to repay their debt.

In many close-knit communities neighbors would come to the aid of each other when disaster struck their homes. In rural communities "barn-raisings" are common events when someone's barn has been destroyed by fire. This kind thing goes on even today.

One of the first insurance exchanges is Lloyd's of London, which has a history that goes back to 1688 when a group of individuals involved in the shipping business began getting together regularly to talk about a variety of issues related to their business including insurance options. Today this insurance exchange serves as a backbone of the insurance industry and manages billions of dollars of insurance premiums transactions.

At the core of all insurance programs, no matter how they work, is protection against events or circumstances that are outside a person's control.

Chapter Two:

WHY WE NEED INSURANCE

We all make plans. Short-term plans may deal with how your day is going to turn out. Long-term plans deal with larger issues like business and life. We all have some notion of how the events in our lives are going to unfold, and take steps towards that vision or away from it. If your plan was to go to work or school today, you probably set an alarm clock so you could wake up, get ready for the day, and head off down the road. The steps you take are consistent with the plans you make.

Luck is an event, usually outside of our control, that we don't plan on. Good luck is an event that helps us realize our personal vision. If the vision was to be at work on time, for instance, and there was much less traffic than normal, you would be happy about your good luck. You planned on there being a certain amount of traffic, and so less traffic, therefore, is a good thing.

Bad luck, on the other hand, is an event that makes it harder to achieve your personal vision. If you got into a horrible traffic jam on the way to work you would probably think it was bad luck.

Every day we experience good and bad luck. We take steps to mitigate the damage caused by bad luck. We check the weather and the traffic report. We don't plan on getting into bad traffic and we take steps to avoid it. If we do get into a jam, we suffer the consequences of being late to work or school. Life goes on.

Minor setbacks are part of life and we all live with them on a daily basis. We experience good luck and bad luck all the time, so things kind of work themselves out. Some events, however, are so significant that they disrupt our long-term plans.

If you planned on retiring at age 65 while continuing to enjoy your current lifestyle, you might take steps now to help make sure that's a reality. You may put money into an IRA or 401K, for instance. If you win the lottery today, you might be able to retire much earlier than you had originally planned. This is good luck in the sense that it helped you realize your long-term vision of the future.

But what if, instead of winning the lottery, you got cancer? Instead of winning millions of dollars, you were sent millions of dollars in medical bills and you lost your ability to work? Or what if your house burned down, leaving you with no place to live and an oppressive mortgage? Now your plan of retiring at age 65 with your current lifestyle might not happen. This, as most people would agree, is bad luck.

Today's insurance policies protect people from the kind of bad luck that can cause major disruptions to long-term plans. It's important to think of these events as bad luck in the sense that they are events outside someone's control, even if they are carefully planned. Furthermore, it's important to note that the kind of bad luck events that insurance covers are the kind of events that no logical person would bring upon themselves even if they could. No rational person would choose to get into a car accident or burn his house down or contract a life-threatening disease.

Of course, some people make choices that may increase the chances that they will experience bad luck. Smokers, for instance, increase the chances that they will contract lung cancer. The smoker isn't choosing lung cancer, but he is choosing a lifestyle that increases the chances of lung cancer. Likewise, people who engage in certain extreme sports are increasing their chances of experiencing bad luck. Nobody would choose to have her bones broken, but she may engage in activities where broken bones are more likely. If she did choose to break her own bones in order to collect insurance it would be fraud, and she could get in big trouble with both the insurance company and the law. More on this later…

Even apparently smart choices can increase the potential for bad luck. People who choose to become doctors, for instance, face the risk of being sued by patients for malpractice, whether valid or not. Doctors don't choose to be sued, but their choice of profession puts them in a position as potential targets for lawsuits.

Airline pilots are more likely to get hurt in a plane crash than other people simply because they are in more planes. They would never choose to crash a plane, but their risk of this type of bad luck is higher nevertheless. Life insurance companies know this and, therefore, charge higher premiums to airline pilots and other people in higher-risk professions.

Similarly, people who choose to live in cities with high crime rates are more likely to fall victim to a crime. No normal person would choose to be the victim of a crime, but a normal person may have a good reason to choose to live in a city with a high crime rate—millions of people do!

Liabilities

A "liability" is a financial obligation arising from a past transaction or event. When bad luck occurs, it often creates a liability. If you cause a car accident with another car, for instance, you may be liable for the other driver's car, medical expenses and other related damages. Your liabilities include the cost of the car, the rental car you drive while your car is being fixed, other property damage, medical bills, and in some cases, the liabilities of others involved.

Nearly all insurance liability settlements provide funds payments to policy holder claimants designed to cover part or all of the liabilities incurred by the policyholder, that is, the insured, as a result of the insured's actions in causing the accident.

In order to be in the insurance business, insurance companies must become experts at predicting the cost of medical expenses, the cost of the repair to vehicles, and the fair compensation to individuals for their pain and suffering that was caused by an auto accident. These are referred to as the insured losses. The insurance company also evaluates the behaviors and choices that the people who caused the auto accident make. This is what makes insurance such a fascinating business!

Chapter Three:

HOW INSURANCE WORKS

On the most basic level, insurance is about sharing the risk of bad luck with a bunch of other people with similar interests. People who are afraid of the losses they might incur if they get into a car accident, for example, buy an insurance policy that will cover their losses if they actually do get into a car accident. In order for this to work, the insurance company has to find a lot of people who want to insure their cars. (Liability insurance is required by law so insurance companies don't have much trouble finding customers!) Everyone pays for his own policy, but only a few actually claim a loss. So the small amounts of money from many cover the large losses of a few. This is, in effect, a "pool" of funds, funds from which victims of bad luck can draw to cover their liabilities in the event of bad luck.

If the insurance company only has a couple of people who pay for policies, it will not be able to accurately estimate their claims if and when they occur. Theoretically, the insurance company could pool the money from car insurance purchasers with the money from other types of insurance. For the most part, insurance companies like to specialize in a few types of insurance because it enables them to properly assess and manage risk. A health insurance company will rarely sell car insurance, for instance.

Risk

In order for insurance companies to know how much to charge someone for coverage, they must become experts in the science of probability. Risk refers to the chances, or probability, of a bad luck event occurring in someone's life. If an insurance company can understand the probability of bad luck, it can create a pricing policy that will allow it to not only cover the losses of policyholders, but also realize a profit so that it can continue to remain in business and provide employees with meaningful jobs.

Let's say 100 people each have a pair of diamond earrings that cost $1000 and they all purchased an insurance policy to replace the earrings if they are lost or stolen. If we assume that 5 percent of the people will lose their earrings or get robbed in any given 12-month period, the total losses will be $5000. So, if the insurance company collected $50 from each of the 100 people, they would have enough to cover the losses that year.

In this simple example, the purchasers of the insurance pooled their money in a way that allowed the five people who actually experienced the bad luck to receive enough money to buy new earrings.

Contrast this with a larger loss such as a fire in your home. In this case, the cost of the insurance is well worth it, given the severity of the loss.

Of course, in this earrings scenario if the insurance company charged only $50 for each of the 100 policies, the company did not make a profit. In fact, they *lost* money. The $5,000 that the insurance company received from the 100 policyholders permitted them to cover the cost of the claims from the 5 policyholders who incurred a loss. The insurance company did not have enough to cover the costs of selling, marketing, and managing the policies, nor did they have enough to investigate and settle the claims. Unless an insurance company takes into account the other costs the business of insurance incurs, the owners of the insurance company will not be pleased!

In practice, only about 45–55 percent of an insurance company's income goes towards paying claims (sometimes as high as 70 percent for certain types of policies); the rest goes to marketing, operations, and profits. This means that the company needs to set prices high enough to cover all these extras. In this earring example, the actual policy price might be closer to $100 instead of $50. This would allow the company to not only pay the claims, but also cover overhead and profits.

Assessing Risk

Even in the super-simple earrings insurance example above, determining the 5 percent probability of bad luck isn't easy. There are many things that could contribute to the potential risk of bad luck. For instance:

- The age of the earrings owner—are younger people more or less prone to getting robbed or losing their earrings than older people?
- The gender of the earrings owner—do boys tend to lose earrings more than girls?
- The owner's involvement in sports—do athletes lose more earrings than non-athletes?
- Travel—do people who travel a lot tend to lose earrings more often?

The list can go on. Each type of insurance has a multitude of circumstances that will impact the chances of a person experiencing bad luck.

For auto insurance the company must take into account many things: age, driving record, gender, history of tickets or accidents, how often the car will be used, where the car will be driven, the purpose of the car, and even the type of car, which can have an impact on the risk.

Chapter Four:

TYPES OF INSURANCE

Pretty much anything that can be lost due to bad luck can be insured, especially if it falls into the category of large and infrequent. There are insurance companies that are willing to consider all kinds of things. Some interesting examples include:

- "Lord of the Dance" Michael Flatley insured his legs for $47 million
- Australian cricketer Merv Hughes insured his moustache for $370,000
- Bruce Springsteen insured his throat for $6 million

- British comedian Ken Dodd insured his teeth for $4.7 million

Insurance companies sell hole-in-one insurance for golf tournaments, weather insurance to brides planning outdoor ceremonies, UFO crash insurance, and even zombie insurance. If you want to be protected from bad luck there are insurance companies out there who will put together a policy. Very specific policies like this are generally referred to as the "London Market" for insurance; Lloyds of London is a key player that specializes in one-off policies to insure one against loss from very unusual events.

Of course, not all insurance companies will issue London Market policies such as zombie insurance. Most specialize in a few major areas of coverage.

One way to think about the types of property/casualty insurance is along two axes. The first axis is whether it's a personal or commercial policy; the second is whether it covers "long-tail" or "short-tail" losses.

Personal vs. Commercial

The difference between personal and commercial insurance policies is fairly straightforward. Personal insurance policies protect people from liabilities incurred as a result of bad luck when doing *personal* things. Commercial insurance policies protect people from liabilities incurred as a result of bad luck when doing *work-related* things. In many cases an individual buys a personal insurance policy and a business buys a commercial policy, but not always. An individual who uses her car for work may need a commercial policy, and a business may buy personal insurance for its employees.

Generally speaking, a commercial activity is one that an individual is paid for. So, giving the kids a ride to school is a *personal* activity, but delivering pizzas for which you get paid is a *commercial* activity.

Short-Tail vs. Long-Tail

A short-tail policy is one that covers events for which losses are relatively easy to predict, and assumes payments are made shortly after the loss occurs. This includes most property insurance, like for cars, homes, buildings, boats, airplanes, and things like that. The cost of replacing a car, for instance, is pretty easy to understand. If you wreck your car, the insurance company can cut you a check pretty fast in an amount that would allow you to get a new, similar car right away.

A long-tail policy, on the other hand, is one that covers events for which the losses are more difficult to predict and may stretch out over a number of years. The cost of settling a class-action lawsuit, for instance, is a long-tail issue. It could take years to settle with all the participants, and the costs could change dramatically over time.

	Short-Tail	Long-Tail
Personal	• Automobile • Homeowners • Renters • Boats • Travel • Shipping • Health	• Home Liability • Umbrella Policies
Commercial	• Automobile (Fleets) • Fire • Theft • Shipping/Cargo • Construction • Travel • Business Continuation • Farming	• Workers Compensation • Product Recalls • Professional Liability • Directors & Officer's Policies • Defamation • Environmental

Additionally, insurance companies tend to specialize in life insurance, non-life insurance (otherwise known as "property and casualty" insurance), and health insurance. Life insurance companies deal with issues related to death and disability. Property and casualty companies deal with losses to property, or medical expenses related to specific events. Health insurance deals with medical-related expenses.

Reinsurance

There is one more type of insurance that is important to understand. Reinsurance is insurance for insurance companies. Insurance companies buy reinsurance policies for the same reason that individuals buy policies: to protect their assets in the event of a loss. In the earring example above, the company expected 5 percent of the people to lose their earrings. But if, for some unforeseen reason, 25 percent of the people lost their earrings, the company would be on the hook for $25,000 in claims—much more than the $5,000 they collected. A reinsurance company would pay part of the claims for the insurance company. Even insurance companies can have bad luck!

It can be helpful to understand the nuances of the types of insurance policies so that when you speak to insurance industry professionals you will sound like you know what you are talking about!

Chapter Five:

WHAT INSURANCE COMPANIES DO

Insurance companies can have lots of employees performing a very wide variety of tasks. Generally speaking, the work they perform falls into the following categories:

- Actuarial
- Underwriting
- Claims Adjusting
- Legal Department
- Investing
- Sales
- Marketing
- Human Resources

- Operations
- Information Technology

Actuarial Department

At the heart of any insurance company is the Actuarial Department. This is the department that decides who and what the company will insure and how much to charge. They gather data from both internal and external sources and analyze it to determine the probability of bad luck, and the potential liabilities associated with that bad luck. The models they build become important assets of the company, and allow it to maintain a competitive advantage. The better a company can predict the probability of losses, the more accurate its pricing can be. If a company charges too much it will lose customers to the competition. If it charges too little it will lose money.

An actuary is a good career for someone who likes math, statistics, economics, anthropology and psychology. And, although there is a lot of science involved, there is plenty of opportunity for creativity. Pricing models and policy limits can be designed to encourage and discourage certain behaviors. For instance, if a health insurance company wants to decrease the amount of claims on certain policies, it can increase the co-pay. The co-pay is the out-of-pocket costs that the policyholder has to pay. If, for instance, a policyholder has to pay 50 percent of the medical bill, he might think twice about going to the emergency room for a splinter!

The Actuarial Department gets to figure out how much to charge for insurance coverage.

Underwriting

When someone wants to buy insurance, it's the Underwriting Department's job to determine how the individual or company falls into the pricing categories defined by the Actuarial Department. They are the people who review the details of a customer's application and related information and decide whether the company wants to insure that customer and, if so, what pricing structure would apply.

The actuaries and the underwriters work closely together to make sure that the right people are being charged the right prices for policies.

Claims Adjusting

An insurance company's reputation is built on its ability to provide good customer service when clients need it the most—when there is a loss. The claims department handles all incoming claims from policyholders and claimants usually through a call center or through field agents. They have to listen to the circumstances of the loss and determine if it is eligible for a funds settlement.

People in the claims department have to have great people skills because they are dealing with people who have just suffered a loss and are likely to be feeling very sensitive. Insurance companies must determine if the terms of the policy were met and the extent of the damage before settling a claim.

In some cases policyholders will attempt to file fraudulent claims. The claims department must be able to figure out who these people are and take the necessary steps to prevent them from collecting, or possibly even prosecute them in certain cases.

The claims department has people in the field who will visit the site of a loss to determine the extent of the damage. They will work one-on-one with policyholders and claimants to make sure they settle the claim as promised. These are the people who show up when your house burns down, or visit with you after a car accident. In some cases they are local agents, in other cases they travel in from remote locations.

Most insurance companies can handle claims over the phone through call centers where claim agents work to settle "short-tail" claims directly with policyholders.

If you enjoy working with people, have good communication skills and can handle potentially stressful situations, you might like working in the claims department of an insurance company.

Sales

Insurance sales agents are the front-line employees of insurance companies, and are responsible for building and maintaining a customer base usually in a specific geographic area or vertical industry. These people have to have the ability to work independently and take the initiative to constantly be on the lookout for new business opportunities. There are over 400,000 insurance agents in the United States alone!

Sales agents must drum up new business by generating new business leads with help from the insurance company's marketing department or through their own efforts. Networking is one of the best ways to find new prospects. Agents get involved in their local community, attend business events, and join groups like the local chamber of commerce or professional organizations. Agents also generate leads online, through direct mail programs and advertising.

In some cases a sales agent may offer insurance policies from a number of different insurance companies. This helps them make sure they get the right policy for their customer at the best price.

Most of the time an insurance sales agent gets paid based on a percentage of the amount that the policyholder pays for the policies he or she sells. This is known as selling on commission and it can be tough at first because you don't have a lot of income coming in. Over the years you will build up a customer base that will renew their policies and you will have regular income. The larger your customer base, the higher your income. Being an insurance sales agent can be very rewarding! A good agent knows it's easier to maintain customer relationships than it is to get new customers, so agents that take care of their customers can earn more and more each year.

The primary jobs in sales are as independent sales agents who represent multiple insurance carriers, and sales agents who are dedicated to one carrier. There are also inside sales reps who sell over the phone, and sales support staff who organize the applications and help the sales agents do their jobs. Sales managers organize the agents and keep track of their progress. At the top of the organization is the Vice President of Sales who is responsible for all the sales activities in the organization.

Marketing

Insurance policies can be very complicated and confusing for consumers. The marketing department of an insurance company needs to create communication programs that help consumers not only understand their insurance options, but also choose one company over another. Some companies market policies directly to consumers through the phone or online; other companies generate sales through a network of agents. Many do both.

Marketing departments in insurance companies play a central role between all functions. They package insurance products to best suit the needs of different target markets. For instance, the marketing department might design a low-cost insurance policy for people with old cars who want basic liability coverage. People with rare collector cars might want a policy that promises to repair, rather than replace, their unique vehicles if possible.

The marketing department will conduct market research to determine which groups of people need insurance policies, and determine if the company has a good option for them. In some cases the company may not want to pursue a particular market.

For instance, an auto insurance company might research the classic car market and learn that in order to serve this particular market they would need to have a deep knowledge of classic cars, access to parts, and relationships with repair shops willing to work on classic cars. They may decide this is too complicated or expensive, and refuse to sell policies to classic car owners.

Once the marketing department has determined the right target market, they will create communication and promotional programs designed to solicit and solidify interest in their policies. This will include websites, online advertising, traditional advertising, sales kits for agents, public relations, television and radio commercials, and anything else that would help to get the word out. Marketing for insurance companies is a great challenge because on the one hand you have to communicate the benefits of a policy quickly, but you also have to make sure you properly communicate the nuances of the policy, including eligibility and legal disclaimers. Insurance is a heavily regulated business so marketers need to have a good understanding of the applicable laws.

There are lots of different jobs in the marketing department, starting with the Chief Marketing Officer (CMO) or Vice President of Marketing. Entry-level jobs include marketing managers, graphic designers, copywriters, marketing associates, social media managers, online marketing managers, event specialists, and a number of others. The marketing department has people who are very creative and some who are very analytical, and everything in between. Few functions in a company are as diverse as marketing; there is always something new!

Legal

Insurance is one of the most regulated industries because it is imperative that they keep the promises they make to policyholders. Regulators keep close watch on the investments and decisions that insurance companies make and the prices they set. Regulators want to make sure that the people who need insurance can get insurance from companies that are going to be around long enough to pay out if there is a loss.

The legal department at an insurance company spends a lot of time dealing with regulators to make sure their requirements are met.

Another important role of the legal department is dealing with potentially fraudulent claims. Because insurance companies write big checks to cover losses there is a high potential for fraud. When the claims department suspects a claim is fraudulent they often involve the legal department.

For instance, workers' compensation claims have historically seen a high volume of fraudulent claims. Fraud investigators review claims, interview policyholders, and may even travel to incidents to collect evidence. A fraud investigator is kind of like a detective.

Insurance companies are always entrenched in legal issues ranging from contract negotiations to trial-room litigation. The legal topics are broad and the cases can be fascinating. Litigation is common in personal injury and business liability cases. Personal injury is when someone is involved in an accident—like a car accident, or slipping on steps. The victim's lawyers will attempt to collect a high settlement; the insurance company's lawyers will attempt to block excessive claims in court. The tobacco industry is often the target of business liability claims arising from alleged misinformation propagated by the tobacco companies with regard to health risks. The settlements are huge, and insurance company lawyers play a central role for both the plaintiff and the defense.

Other legal functions include efforts to help shape the laws through government lobbying on the federal, state, and local levels. Insurance companies spend a lot of money and effort creating the right legal landscape in which to operate. Health insurance companies are on high alert as congress votes on healthcare reform laws. The outcomes of congressional votes can have a huge impact on the insurance company's ability to do business.

At the state level, auto insurance companies lobby state senators with regard to speed limits and traffic laws. In response to oil embargoes in the early 1970s, the Nixon administration mandated lower speed limits as a way of saving gas. The mandate was lifted in 1987. Since then many states have increased speed limits to as high as 80 mph or more. Insurance companies watch the effects of these changes very carefully, and advise lawmakers to enact laws that create a good environment for insurance coverage. On the one hand higher speeds lead to more severe accidents and higher rates of injury or death; but on the other hand matching the speed limit to what most drivers operate at anyway may reduce the number of accidents. These kinds of challenges keep the insurance industry interesting!

Insurance companies hire not only lawyers, but also paralegals, clerks, and administrative assistants.

Information Technology (IT)

Insurance companies have some of the most sophisticated technology systems of any companies. Insurance companies have a lot of information and need a lot of computing power to manage and analyze the data. There are a number of major components to IT as described below.

Consumer-Facing Programs

Any system that a consumer would interact with is a consumer-facing program. This includes websites, apps, or other programs to help policyholders shop for or manage their policies.

Consumer-facing programs support the marketing department, and should integrate well with other communication programs. Some insurance companies consider the Internet to be their primary channel for sales and don't maintain an agent network. In other cases the company provides online tools for their agent network that will search for information and pricing on behalf of their clients.

Marketing and Sales Information Systems

Closely related to the consumer-facing programs are the information systems behind them that keep track of all the applications and data, and provide access for all the departments that touch the policy such as accounting, actuarial, underwriting, customer service, claims, billing, and marketing.

The back-end information systems provide important data to the company's employees for analysis. Using this data they can learn things about their customers, including:

- Most popular policies
- Average sale price
- Sales agent performance
- Most productive advertising efforts

Marketers slice and dice the data in all sorts of ways to ensure that they invest their marketing dollars in the most productive way.

Actuarial Data Systems

Insurance actuaries need access to huge amounts of data compiled from different sources. The IT department maintains sophisticated database systems for them that provide access to statistical data on everything the company might insure.

Actuaries working on automobile insurance are most interested in the company's internal claims data, and may supplement this with data from the Department of Transportation, local law enforcement, automobile safety data, and third-party research. The IT department assists the actuary in accessing this data.

Actuaries working on homeowners insurance are also most interested in the company's internal claims data and may supplement this with data on home prices, crime rates, construction prices, weather patterns, and other information that will help them predict the rates for homeowners insurance

Tech Support

One of the core functions of any IT department is providing the right equipment and support to employees and agents in the field. Most insurance company employees interact with a computer, laptop, tablet, smartphone, or other technology appliance on a daily basis. The IT department provides this equipment and makes its team available to employees who have problems.

There are lots of different jobs in IT at an insurance company. The most senior person is the Chief Information Officer (CIO) or Chief Technology Officer (CTO). There are jobs for programmers, designers, user interface experts, database administrators, application architects, systems engineers, quality assurance analysts, networking professionals, and customer service representatives.

Investing

Remember that insurance is essentially a pool of funds from which people who suffer property damage or bodily injury may receive compensation from applicable insurance coverage. Part of the policy premiums that the insured pays goes into this pool where it is available when needed to pay claims. However, the insurance company gets to invest a lot of these funds to keep policy premiums lower and to achieve the profit targets of the insurance company. Investment income is an important factor in setting rates for insurance policies.

Insurance companies invest these funds into all kinds of things. One of the most popular investments are bonds. This keeps the money safe—in case the company needs it to pay claims—but allows it to make money at the same time.

Of course, you would think that all investments are intended to get maximum returns for minimal risk. And they are, but hedge funds take this to another level altogether using investment techniques that require lots of funds. For instance, a hedge fund manager might execute a lot of trades during certain events. This requires them to have the funds available to make those trades. Or they might want to spread money across global markets in a lot of different sectors. You can't do this kind of thing unless you have a lot of funds.

Hedge funds aren't the only investment option insurance companies utilize. They also invest in more traditional investments and they will even keep some money in very safe investments like treasury bills. The investment group at an insurance company does what it can to turn that giant pool of funds into an ever bigger pile of funds so they can keep rates affordable and realize higher profits.

The investment group of an insurance company tends to hire people with a financial background who know how to analyze a variety of investment tools such as stocks, bonds, options, commodities, treasury notes, and other financial tools. Entry-level analysts do research and prepare reports for senior managers.

Human Resources

The main functions of the Human Resource (HR) department are recruiting employees, managing payroll and benefits for those employees, providing training and development opportunities, and handling the departure of employees who leave the company voluntarily or otherwise.

Recruiting

Large insurance companies are always interested in attracting talented, motivated employees. Members of the HR team scour the globe looking for the right employees. Later in this book you will learn more about how to be the kind of person they are looking for, and how to design your strategy for getting your foot in the door.

Recruiters make heavy use of the Internet for finding candidates. There are a lot of popular job sites where recruiters can post openings. LinkedIn.com is a professional networking site. Because profiles contain professional information instead of social information, it is a great place for recruiters to hang out online.

In addition to online searches, recruiters will have recruiting events such as job fairs or on-campus programs where they are able to meet directly with potential candidates. These events are great ways for them to learn about candidates on a personal level, even if it's only for a few minutes.

Payroll and Benefits Administration

One of the main reasons anyone works for any company is the expectation of receiving compensation in the form of salary and benefits. In a large insurance company there might be a lot of employees, and keeping everything organized takes a lot of work. Benefit and payroll administrators make sure each employee is getting paid the right amount with the right taxes taken out, and with the right amount going into 401K programs or other retirement programs. Additionally, they make sure that each person is properly enrolled in health insurance and other benefits programs that the company might offer.

Sometimes companies offer training opportunities, memberships to health clubs and wellness programs, opportunities to participate in charitable events, and various other benefits.

Outplacement

When an employee leaves a company, whether voluntarily or not, the HR department manages the departure. The staff must let the departing employee know about the termination of her benefits and how she can continue some of the benefits, if applicable. For instance, in most cases the employee will be entitled to continue health coverage under a program called COBRA. In some cases the employee will be eligible for unemployment benefits.

When a person leaves a company, the circumstances under which he leaves may have an impact on what ongoing benefits he will have access to. If he is fired, for instance, he may not be eligible for unemployment insurance. If he is laid off, however, he may be eligible for unemployment benefits as well as other benefits. Some companies offer outplacement services which provide job search support such as resume and interview help, temporary office space, and job search coaching.

While some jobs in HR require specialized skills such as counseling, most of them can be learned on the job. An interest in helping people is a key qualification. The most senior position in HR is usually the Vice President of Human Resources. Other jobs include payroll specialists, recruiters, and benefits managers.

Other Important Functions

Other than the above, insurance companies do a lot of things that other companies do. The accounting group makes sure that policyholders pay their premiums and that the bills get paid. The facilities group makes sure they all have a safe place to work. Some jobs are specific to the insurance industry and some require skills that are relevant to all industries.

Some health insurance companies keep registered nurses or even physicians on staff to help them develop ways to keep their clients healthy, or to answer simple health-related questions over the phone. This helps keep people out of the doctor's office and out of the hospital unless absolutely necessary. This reduces the number of claims filed, and therefore, the amount of money the insurance company has to spend on claims.

A health insurance company might have its own mail-order pharmacy. An auto insurance company might have close relationships with parts distribution companies. A cell phone insurance company probably maintains an inventory of replacement phones for policyholders. These kinds of services are all designed to help the company better service customers and save money.

Insurance is big business and insurance companies need thousands of employees to keep it all going. There are always job openings at insurance companies, and if you play your cards right you can have one!

Chapter Six:

JOBS IN INSURANCE

The best way to learn about what goes on inside an insurance company is from the inside. This means you will have to get a job in an insurance company. The good news is that insurance companies are *always* hiring. They are always on the lookout for talent and there is no reason why you can't get a job in insurance.

Please note that much of the advice outlined in this book applies to finding a job in any industry, but we have been sure to emphasize how it applies to insurance.

The first step in the process is to figure out which foot you're going to put in which door. Clearly you want to put your best foot forward and I'll show you a few ways to do that. *Which* door is a little more complicated—the insurance industry has lots of doors!

Earlier I described what insurance companies do, including actuarial, underwriting, processing claims, investing, sales, marketing, human resources, operations, and information technology. There are a variety of entry-level jobs within each of these functional areas. What's especially cool about the insurance industry is that no matter where you start, you can create your own career path once you get in the door. There are endless possibilities. The insurance industry is so big that there is plenty of mobility. The skills you develop in one department will probably be applicable across a variety of departments. So, if you join the underwriting group and you don't like it, moving to the marketing group is a real possibility. You can stay in the insurance industry for your entire career, but you can move through a very diverse variety of jobs within the industry.

The first step is to create your strategy for which doors you want to pursue. No matter what you majored in in college, it has probably prepared you for a career in insurance. Not too many industries can make that claim!

Jobs by Major

College Major	Entry-Level Jobs
Accounting	Underwriting, Accounting, Finance, Claims
Business/Management	Sales, Marketing, Customer Service, Human Resources
Computer Science	Information Technology, Marketing, Underwriting
Economics	Sales, Marketing, Underwriting, Claims
Finance	Investing, Finance, Accounting, Underwriting, Claims
Liberal Arts	Sales, Marketing, Customer Service, Human Resources, Claims
Math	Actuarial, Underwriting, Finance, Accounting, Claims

In the insurance industry there is always demand for people who have quantitative skills like math, science, engineering, and technology. These people help design insurance products that make money for the company while offering a good value to the customer.

Likewise, there is always demand for people who have qualitative skills—like effective communications skills (both written and oral), design skills, and comprehensive reading skills. These people can work successfully in marketing, sales, customer service, human resources and even information technology. The insurance business has a place for everyone.

Career Path

Every department has entry-level positions. At the lower levels of an organization the main focus is on *doing*. Your first few jobs in an insurance company will have you doing things like answering calls from customers, designing brochures, analyzing data, or entering payments or revenue into an accounting system. Your ability to do these things effectively (without mistakes) and efficiency (quickly) will in large part determine your ability to grow within the organization.

As your experience and expertise grows, you may have the opportunity to compete for a supervisory or managerial position, if you so desire. In these roles your job is to manage other people who are doing the work. So, instead of fielding customer phone calls, for instance, you would be managing a group of people who take calls. Your job would be to make sure your team is properly trained and to make sure they are happy and productive. You will set goals for them and meet with them regularly to see how they are progressing towards those goals.

When you move further up the ladder you will direct other managers. Your job will be to make sure the managers and employees are doing what the senior management team wants them to do. Your main functions will be communication-based, where you interact with different levels of the organization and make sure everyone is on the same page.

Eventually you will grow into a more senior-level position where planning and leadership are more important. You will design systems and programs that can be implemented by employees that will help the company achieve the vision of the organization. You will create spending plans and budgets and other plans that your department will execute for you.

The top managers in an insurance company are there to chart the right path for the organization, and to inspire them to take action along that path. You will deal on a high level with the direction of the market and the economy as a whole. It takes years to become experienced enough to take a senior leadership position in an insurance company, but the rewards are very high. So... let's start with that entry-level position.

Chapter Seven:

FINDING A JOB

Most people spend hours surfing Internet job boards for job postings, submit their resumes, and then wonder why they aren't getting showered with job offers. This is not the best approach. There are lots of ways to approach your job search, but the important thing is to create some structure and process around everything, so that you are always moving the ball forward.

Prepare Your Pitch

One of the first things you will want to do is create a personal sale pitch—who you are, what you do, what makes you unique, why you are valuable, etc. Spend some time on this step. You will want to be able to present yourself to prospective employers confidently. You should do this first because you never know when you are going to meet someone who can help you get to where you want to go. If you don't know what you are going to say to these people, I can guarantee you will say the wrong thing. If a recruiter from a great insurance company called you today to tell you about a job opening, what would you say to that person about why you are the right person for the job? You probably have no idea.

Your pitch should be a quick 30-second synopsis of who you are, and what you are all about. It's kind of like a movie trailer. It doesn't tell the whole story, but it tells enough so that people want to learn more. Here are a few examples:

> *My name is Sally Smith. I have a bachelor's degree in mathematics from [College] where I focused on statistics. I've always loved numbers and I'm eager to find a way to make a positive contribution to a company in statistical analysis. I would love to work my way into the actuarial department of an insurance company as a junior actuary. I think my passion for statistics and my interest in business would make me a great fit.*

Or…

My name is John Doe, I'm a design major from [College] and I'm looking for an opportunity to help companies communicate complex issues in simple, straightforward ways that appeal to an individual's emotions. I've had my eye on the insurance business for some time. The right communication program can really connect with customers and help them better understand their insurance options. I worked on an insurance campaign for one of my classes and really enjoyed the project. I think I can add a lot to a design and marketing team.

Or…

My name is Jane Doe, I was a history and sociology major at [College]. I found the whole field of human behavior fascinating and I'm interested in finding ways to use this passion to make a positive contribution in a corporate environment. I'm very curious about becoming an insurance claims adjuster because I love working with people and helping them solve their problems.

These are all pretty good pitches. All three of them provide a little background and connect it to providing real value at an insurance company. They communicate passion, energy, and a willingness to make a positive contribution.

Other materials you produce—like your resume, cover letters, thank-you notes, personal blog, etc.—should support the messages. You want people to instantly understand who you are and what you stand for professionally.

Sink Your Hook

When you meet someone in the industry who might be a connection, you will want to be prepared with your pitch. It should be delivered smoothly and naturally. Write it down and practice in front of the mirror.

In order to sink your hook, you will need some follow-up questions that you can ask to further solidify the person's interest in you. The best way to make them interested in *you* is for you to show an interest in *them*. People love to talk about themselves and you will want to make sure that you let them do this while you absorb what they say with genuine interest. Here is a list of questions that you can ask to get people to talk about themselves:

- ✓ *How did you get involved in the insurance industry?*
- ✓ *What does your department do?*
- ✓ *What interests you about the insurance industry?*
- ✓ *What kinds of things did you do early in your career to get ahead?*
- ✓ *What makes your company different from other insurance companies?*

Armed with your pitch and a list of good follow-up questions, you are ready to move on to the next step: uncovering opportunity.

Uncovering Opportunity

There are two kinds of jobs—those that are posted on job boards all over the Internet that every Tom, Dick and Harry are applying to, and those that are not posted at all. You actually have a better chance of landing a job that is *not* listed on the Internet. However, it is much easier to find jobs that are listed on the Internet. This means that although your chances are lower of landing one, you will have many more chances. So, looking for jobs on the Internet will be part of your regular routine.

Start with search sites like *Monster.com* and *SimplyHired.com*. Keep an open mind, and search on a national basis. Keep your options as broad as possible. Take note of any jobs that look interesting and set them aside. Do whatever you need to do to stay organized. You can use a Customer Relationship Management (CRM) program as a contact manager. There are free or inexpensive versions online. Try Zoho.com for a pretty good option.

Next, search the job boards from your college or graduate school. These are gold mines. Search Craigslist.org. Search industry association sites. Search everywhere and set aside jobs that look interesting to you.

When you have searched for an hour or so, stop and review what you have. Don't worry, there will be plenty of new jobs to find tomorrow.

Non-Published Jobs

For every job you find online, there are probably a lot more that are not online. These haven't been posted because the company hasn't gotten around to it yet, or maybe they aren't even aware it needs to be filled. There are lots of managers out there who need people, but simply haven't taken the steps necessary to get the HR department to formally post the position. Many of these jobs are filled by internal candidates or by people the hiring manager already knows. You will uncover these jobs through networking and reaching out to people in the industry.

When you identify jobs either online or through networking, simply submitting your resume isn't enough. You need to infiltrate the company and get to know the company, the job, and the people from all angles.

Pick the jobs that sound like jobs you want to have—no big revelation here, I know. But you shouldn't get desperate and apply to anything and everything; it's discouraging and a waste of time. Find one or two jobs that you would like to concentrate on for today and set the others aside.

Networking

Your next step is to find people you know who know the people hiring for the positions you are interested in. You want to get near the people who are near the hiring manager. Not the HR manager, the *hiring* manager—the person who will actually be making the final decision. There are three great resources for this that I have found. The first is your brain—who do you know? The second is your alumni database. The third are social networking sites, especially LinkedIn.com.

Your Brain

You probably know a lot more people than you think. These people make up your personal network and even the average person will have connections he or she never even realized. If the job you are reviewing is in the same geographic area where you live, you are bound to be only a few degrees of separation from the hiring manager.

Make a list of everyone you know—everyone. Start with your friends, people you used to work with, classmates, people from church or the club or your sports group or anything. You will really have to think about this. If you can't remember someone's name, write down "that dude with the red hair who drives a Jeep," or something else to remind you. For each person, try to summarize the network he or she has. For instance:

- **Peter Parker**, photographer, knows newspaper editors, super hero, kind of a loner, nerd, may know people in science, close with professors, totally whipped by his next-door neighbor.

Ah, now you remember his neighbor—what was her name?

- Peter Parker's next-door neighbor. Jane? **Mary Jane**? She was a waitress, wanted to act, was in that play, may know the owner of the theater, probably knows actors and writers, dated super-wealthy guy whose father was in the weapons businesses, something chemical.

Ah-ha, now you remember the super-wealthy guy:

- Mary Jane is friends with **Harry Osborn** whose dad develops weapons. They have a lot of other investments; one of them is Osinsure, a subsidiary of Oscorp. He is well-connected through the family business, but he is also friends with Peter Parker.

Do this for the hundred or so people you know and you will not only remember others, but you will soon see a path to the door of probably 70 percent of the people you are trying to reach. Now, let's say you want to get a job at Osinsure. You could call Peter who can introduce you to Harry who can introduce you to someone who works at Osinsure. Or perhaps he knows someone else you can call. You will hit dead ends, but this is part of the process. You would be shocked at the number of connections you have. You're probably only one or two degrees away from the right person.

Alumni Databases

Just about every university in the country has an online alumni database. This is a huge resource. You will use it every day. The nice part about these databases is that you can search by employers, towns, profession, and a slew of other criteria that can help you hone your search. Don't hesitate to contact fellow alumni:

> *Hello, Joe? My name is Sally Smith. I found your name in the [College] alumni database and I'm contacting you because I saw that you work for Osinsure, Inc. I came across a job positing for a job in underwriting and I was*

wondering if you have a few minutes to tell me a little about the company before I apply?

Or…

Hello, Joe? My name is Sally Smith. I found your name in the [College] alumni database and I'm contacting you because I saw that you work for Osinsure, Inc. I'm interested in starting my career in the insurance industry and I was wondering if you have a few minutes to tell me a little about the company.

(Chit-chat…)

Thank you so much for your time. **Would you be able to make an introduction to the hiring manager so I can reach out to her personally?**

Simple as that!

Social Networking Sites

Facebook.com and LinkedIn.com are the two networks that you will use most often. LinkedIn.com is probably the best. If you don't already have a LinkedIn.com account, then take a moment to set one up. Search for your friends, associates, classmates and everyone else from your list. Build your network far and wide.

Social network sites have groups where people talk about all sorts of things including job opportunities. Be sure to wear your spam boots for wading through some serious junk, but a little digging can uncover some real opportunities.

Be sure to make sure your profiles on both Facebook.com and LinkedIn.com portray you as a mature professional and not a crazy college kid. If you have had a history of posting pictures of yourself scantily clad at parties, you may want to go back and delete anything that might cast you in an unprofessional light.

Connecting

The point of all this networking is to find people close to the job you want so you can call them and get the inside scoop on what the company and the job is all about. *You are not trying to get them to put in a good word for you,* so don't ask. If they like you they may put in a good word, but the real point of talking to them is to help you decide if you will *let them* hire you. They have to be the right place. Don't be cocky, be inquisitive.

You want to network yourself closer and closer to the actual hiring manager. When you ultimately reach that person you can contact him or her directly. Far fewer people do this than you might think.

> *Hello, Hank hiring manager, my name is Sally Smith. Harry Osborne gave me your name and told me a little about the opening for a position in your underwriting department. I'm very interested in learning more. I've researched your company and it looks like a great place. I noticed that you launched a new line of interesting products a few weeks ago and I was very impressed. I'd love to be part of a team that creates these offerings…*

When they ask you about yourself:

> *I have a bachelor's degree in mathematics from [College] where I focused on statistics. I've always loved numbers and I'm eager to find a way to make a positive contribution to a company in statistical analysis. I would love to work my way into the underwriting department of an insurance company as a junior actuary. I think my passion for statistics and my interest in business would make me a great fit. Osinsure sounds like an ideal place, and I would love to learn more about the position…*

Once you build a little rapport with the person you can ask a series of questions that will come in handy when you sit down and write a cover letter. You will want to ask things like:

- ✓ *Why is the position open? Is it new or a replacement?*
- ✓ *Why did the previous person leave?*
- ✓ *Why was the position created?*
- ✓ *What changes do you hope the next person will bring?*
- ✓ *How central to the company's overall strategy is this role?*
- ✓ *What other departments are affected by this role?*
- ✓ *What do you hope to accomplish over the next few years?*

And so on, until you have a good feel for what the person is looking for. Then you can end like this:

> *I really appreciate all this great information. I am definitely interested in applying. May I have your email address so I can follow up with some additional detail?*

> *Thank you so much. I'll give you a ring next week to talk about next steps. I look forward to meeting you.*

You will say these things *even if you think the job sounds like a drag.* Always go for the offer. You can always turn it down, but always go for the offer. Do your hemming and hawing later.

Other Research

Aside from networking your way into the company you will also want to do plenty of research on the job, the company, the people, and anything else you can find. Read, read, read. The more you know, the better your introductory letter will be.

Keep track of the information you find by keeping it in a folder on your computer. Keep a copy of all your research. Volume counts. Later, when you interview, you will print it out and take it all with you to the interview in neatly-labeled file folders. More on this later.

PRESENTING YOURSELF

After you have done your research and made the necessary connections, you will be ready to sit down and apply to one job per day. Do not apply to more than one job per day. You can research as many jobs as you want. You can follow up on as many jobs as you want. But you may only apply to one job per day. This is important.

Some people apply to dozens of jobs per day, even hundreds. They send out emails haphazardly and fill out a bunch of online application forms—a complete and utter waste of time.

First of all, applying to dozens of jobs means you will get rejected from dozens of jobs, which is demoralizing. The whole process is depressing—filling out online forms, cutting and pasting your resume into text fields, etc. It's horrible. If you come across a job that only accepts applications this way, skip it. The only time you should fill out an online application form is when someone asks you to do so as part of the application process. Unless you've made contact with the company and sent them a letter first, filling out their online application is just a waste of time.

Applying for a job is an important step. It is your application letter that will make or break your chances of getting an interview. The *letter* is the important factor. The resume is a killer—do not send a resume!

Don't Send Your Resume

Contrary to what you might have been told, there is nothing that will *kill* your chances of getting an interview faster than sending a resume. Resumes *do not* get interviews. They are horrible marketing tools. Do not send one if you can avoid it. The only time you should send a resume is if they specifically ask for one as part of your advancement to the next phase of the interview process. Even then it is risky. The best time to present a resume is at the interview itself.

I know this is counterintuitive advice. After all, a carefully crafted resume is a key document in the job search process. But the fact is that your resume looks like the hundreds of other resumes that the person will see that day. It will get two seconds of time (if that) before it is discarded.

Your resume, like everyone else's resume, is sprinkled with buzz words and action words. Resumes, for people applying to the same job, are all the same. You can't differentiate yourself very well with a resume. This does not mean that resumes aren't important. They are very important. It just means that *how* you use them and *when* you introduce them into the process is more important.

A well-written introductory letter, on the other hand, can and will make you stand out. Once you understand this simple truth, your job search will be much more productive. Think of your resume as an outline. This outline will be used to write your letter and it will be used to conduct your interview. It is a tool to help you keep your story straight because everyone gets a different spin. Your resume will help you put on the correct spin and keep track of what you are saying.

The Letter

The letters you write to your future employer are the keys to getting through the interview process. Write them well and you are in. Write them half-heartedly and you might as well not write them at all.

The reason I recommend the rule of applying to one job per day is because all your energy should be going into the one perfect letter that will land you the interview. It's too easy to cut and paste your "cover letter" into emails and online forms. However, a well-written letter will pave the way.

Your letter will include some of the important things you learned about the company during your research and from conversations with other employees. It will also highlight important aspects of your experience that tie neatly into the needs of the company. Lastly, it will make a personal connection with the reader so that he or she will like you and want to interview you.

Your resume, which you will not send, is sort of like an outline for your letter. Your letter should reflect the important parts of your resume.

Dear Hank,

It was a pleasure speaking with you yesterday about your opening for a junior actuary. I find your company fascinating. You mentioned that one of your challenges was leveraging social networking and other new media to capture data to build risk profiles, and that you wanted some real out-of-the-box thinking. It may interest you to know that as part of a class project I created a statistical analysis of data scraped from Facebook pages to determine the most popular song in a 24-hour period. The model was very accurate and allowed us to predict how Facebook users would respond to new songs by similar artists. I realize that popular songs and insurance risk are different things, but I think this is a good example of how I have applied statistical models to solve problems.

You mentioned that you were looking for someone who is not only good at statistics, but also isn't afraid to pitch in and work with a team. Nearly all of my projects in school have been team projects, and I've averaged extremely high on peer reviews.

Your job description listed several requirements for the position including a bachelor's degree in mathematics, at least one year of experience, and a solid understanding of technology. I received a BS from [College] and spent two summers as a research assistant for PhD students doing a variety of modeling tasks. Both of my supervisors would be happy to speak with you about my performance and contribution.

Based on my conversations with you, Peter, John, and Francine, I am quite confident that I could be a solid member of your team. I also believe that I could be making a meaningful contribution in a very short term, given my previous exposure to some of your current challenges.

I would really enjoy the opportunity to meet with you and other members of your team in person. I can be reached at (773) 555-5391 or via email at sally@stateu.edu. I look forward to meeting you.

Most sincerely,

Sally Smith

This is a good letter. It is very relevant to the needs of the organization, it shows that you have done your homework, it demonstrates a genuine ability to fulfill the requirements of the position, and it expresses sincere interest in the company. It isn't short, but it's not too long either. Your job is to write a better letter than any other application letter the person has ever received, or will ever receive, in his entire career. This may sound like a tall order, but it's not. The overwhelming majority of introductory cover letters are horrible.

Once in my personal career, I got an unsolicited application letter that really stood out. I didn't have a job opening at the time but I did invite the candidate to lunch. And, although she wasn't as interesting as her letter, I did help her out with some personal referrals, and I have kept in touch with her over the years. It is amazing what a good letter will accomplish. By the way, you can email your letter, you don't have to handwrite it.

This letter will serve as your application for the job. However, you have not fulfilled your "apply to one job" obligation until you write equally compelling letters to everyone you spoke to at the company. This may take a few hours, but it is time well spent. If you try to apply to more than one job per day you will not have time to give each application the attention it deserves. In the job-hunting game, *quality* is much more important than *quantity*. Most people do the opposite. You won't (I hope).

Following Up

If it's been a day or two since you sent your letters and they haven't responded, they will need a reminder. If they are anything like most people at work, then their email box is an abyss. Your reminder will be welcomed by them. You can send a nice, quick reminder every two or three days until you hear back. Make sure your most recent letter is below your reminder note.

Hi Hank,

I'm just checking in to see if you have had time to review the letter I sent a few days ago. If the position for the junior actuary is still open I would still like to get together to talk in more detail. I have some availability later this week on Thursday or Friday. Let me know if either of those days work for you. I can be reached at (773) 555-5391 or via email at sally@college.edu.

Sincerely,

Sally

You can send as many notes as you want. Quantity is rarely a problem, but frequency is. Don't send them every day; you need to give the person a chance to respond. You will know it's time to stop when one of three things happen:

1. They tell you the position has been filled
2. They tell you that they don't want you
3. You have accepted a new job

If they tell you that they don't think you are a good "fit" for the job, you probably didn't do enough research or wrote a bad letter. Your research is intended to give you an understanding of what a good fit looks like, and your letter is to let them know that you look like the good fit. Of course, you may not be a good fit, in which case you wouldn't get the job no matter how good your letter was.

If you truly think you are a good fit, you don't have to give up. You can write another letter with a different spin. It is possible to reignite interest in your application. The company might appreciate your being persistent and not taking no for an answer. Getting someone to reconsider you after they said "no" is a great feeling. It builds confidence along the way. That being said, don't beat a dead horse!

The Interview

When you accept an interview your goal is to get the offer even if you decide that you don't want the job during the interview process. I say this because it is easy to sabotage yourself if the job doesn't look like something you are interested in. Go for the offer; you can always turn it down. In this game, you are playing to win, not to place or show.

This means you will have to not only present yourself in a way that is compatible with the needs of the organization, but also you will want people to like you. Both of these things require two underused skills: listening and asking questions.

No matter what is going on in your life, you want to walk into the room and present an air of confidence and poise. Your presence in the room must win them over. You must dress the part, say the right things, and use the right body language.

The purpose of an interview is to *position* yourself as the best candidate. This isn't to say that you want to pretend to be someone you're not. You will be honest with your presentation of yourself, but you will want to make sure you are hitting the right hot-buttons so that your candidacy will rise to the top.

This means that sitting down to answer a bunch of questions is probably not the best strategy. This may sound counterintuitive. After all, the interviewer is trying to get to know you. However, you must first get to know the interviewer.

To get to know him or her, you must have the opportunity to ask a few questions of your own. If the interviewer starts in right away, you have to stop him by saying, "Before I answer, do you mind if I ask you a few questions about the position so I can be sure that my answers are relevant?"

Asking this question will do more for your credibility than just about anything else you say during the interview. You have shown that you are interested in the position, and you have turned the tables and taken control of the interview process and will be able to steer it in a direction that will help you look good.

What to Wear

Always dress one notch more formally than the regular company dress code. This means that you will have to find out, in advance, what people wear. It's okay to ask any one of your contacts something like, "How do people typically dress at Osinsure?"

If they wear:	You wear:
Shorts and T-shirts	Nice jeans and a polo shirt
Jeans and polo shirts	Slacks and a dress shirt
Slacks and a dress shirt	Slacks and a dress shirt and a blazer
Slacks and a dress shirt and a blazer	Suit
Suit	Dark suit

Most insurance companies dress professionally; some departments, like sales, will be more formal than others. When in doubt, wear a suit with a light-colored shirt.

What to Bring

Before your interview, find out how many people you will be meeting and bring at least that number of copies of your resume plus a couple of extras. If you have a portfolio or samples of previous work (especially if you are applying for a marketing position), bring your best work. If you are applying for a sales position, bring copies of thank-you notes from previous clients (if you have them).

Lastly, remember the research you did earlier? Bring copies of all of your research in neatly-labeled file folders. You will not explicitly show these documents to your interviewers, but make sure they are visible during the interview. This concrete evidence that you took the time to prepare for the interview will leave a very positive impression on everyone you meet. What better evidence that you will be an organized and well-prepared employee than being an organized and well-prepared candidate?

What to Ask

Earlier I mentioned some questions that you might ask the hiring manager:

- ✓ *Why is the position open? Is it new or a replacement?*
- ✓ *Why did the previous person leave?*
- ✓ *Why was the position created?*
- ✓ *What changes do you hope the next person will bring?*
- ✓ *How central to the company's overall strategy is this role?*
- ✓ *What other departments are affected by this role?*
- ✓ *What do you hope to accomplish over the next few years?*

These questions are fair game in all interviews, but you don't want to ask the same persons to repeat themselves so be sure to take notes on who answers what.

What to Say and What Not to Say

Be sure to cast yourself in the best possible light, and show enthusiasm and excitement for the position. Talk about specific accomplishments you have had, not about how hard you work. Nobody cares how hard you work; they only care about your results.

Never talk about people you don't like, and never blame anyone for your personal shortcomings. This sounds obvious, but gossip is so common in our social lives that you might mistake the interviewer for a friend and start heading down the wrong path.

Talk about your passions and your interests, but be sure to tie them back to the job. It's easy to get sidetracked talking about hobbies. Avoid discussions about politics, religion or anything that is illegal.

If you have ever been fired from a former job and you are asked to explain why, do so simply and succinctly. Be sure to sum it up with what you learned as a result. You may want to practice this answer so it comes across properly. The last thing you want to do is get into a long story about your failure. The only thing worse than that is to blame your former boss (even if it is his or her fault)!

Taking Notes

During your interview you will want to take plenty of notes. The reason you take notes is so you can go home and write a nice, relevant, and engaging thank-you note to the interviewer. You will be looking for things that he seems to care about, or things he said that you thought were rather insightful. You will be looking for his hot-buttons, and your thank-you note will give you another opportunity to address them. Jot down notes about his most important goals, corporate values, and company culture; even the interviewer's hobbies can become great thank-you note fodder.

Body Language

How you use your body, your non-verbal communication, is critical to your success. In fact, it is probably more important than what you actually say. Most people will have forgotten what you say by the time you walk out the door. However, the impression you left on them will last.

When it comes to body language you have to master the art of *mirroring*. Mirroring is replicating the body language of the interviewer—unless the interviewer is crossing her arms. If the interviewer leans forward, pause a moment and then lean forward yourself. If she leans back, pause a moment and then lean back. She uses her arms? You use your arms.

Mirroring has a powerful non-verbal effect on people. It makes them believe that the two of you are on the same page. It builds a positive rapport and it makes you memorable. When someone feels a physical connection (not sexual) and feels listened to, he or she will remember the interaction very positively.

Never, ever, cross your arms. When you cross your arms you lose all credibility. Worse, you close yourself off from new ideas and suggestions. You send a message that you don't care what the other person is talking about. Your energy level drops and the enthusiasm is sucked out of the room.

If you find that the interviewer's arms are crossed, you can bet whatever you're saying isn't coming across the way you intend, or in a way that will help you get a job. When this happens, you must get him to uncross his arms. You can do this by handing him something, like your résumé, or by adjusting your message to something more on-topic, or something that reflects the interviewer's point of view. You will know this because you were listening and taking notes.

Be mindful of other basic rules of etiquette. Smile, say "please" and "thank you," look people in the eye, and use a firm handshake. These things are simple enough, but they are easy to forget when you are nervous.

Follow-Up

When you get back home, you will want to sit back down and write some nice thank-you notes to everyone you met. You will know what to write because you took lots of notes. In fact, most of your note-taking is intended specifically for the purpose of writing a good thank-you note.

Dear Hank,

It was really nice meeting you today and learning more about Osinsure. I left your office very excited about the prospect of working there and I sincerely hope we can continue our conversation.

I was especially intrigued with our conversation about risk models built using Facebook.com profiles and how your team was able to gather data by analyzing profile images. As you suggested, I went through some of my friends' profiles and saw some of the issues you mentioned. It's a real eye-opener! I'm glad my profile image didn't put me in the "high risk" category!

You mentioned that this position involves quite a bit of travel. I want to assure you that the travel is not an issue for me. In fact, I consider the travel a benefit of the job as I enjoy visiting new places and working with new people.

With regard to the certification course you mentioned, I'm sure I can complete the course before the start of summer with no problems.

Thank you very much for your time and consideration. I look forward to hearing from you soon!

Most sincerely,

Sally Smith

PS: I'm going to keep an eye out for that restaurant you mentioned in Seattle next time I'm there!

This note is professional, but also personal. It draws on specific details from the conversation, which really shows the interviewer that this person was paying attention. If you don't hear back from the company, then continue to follow up until they tell you to stop or until they send you an offer letter!

Chapter Eight:

STARTING YOUR NEW JOB

The first step in starting your new job is agreeing to the terms in your offer letter. Make sure you are happy with what they are offering and ask for what you want. It will never be easier to negotiate a better deal than right now. Some terms of your offer are more negotiable than others. It's okay to ask. Entry-level jobs in the insurance industry don't have a lot of wiggle room. The structure is usually set by the human resource department. Your best bet is to try to negotiate a higher salary.

Term	How to Negotiate
Base Salary	There is often a salary range that can be offered for the position. Salary limits are often dependent on title. You can (and should) ask for a little more money if you want to. In most cases you will get it. If the offer is much lower than you expected, you may have to negotiate a job with more responsibility (if you think you can handle it).
Title	Job titles in larger companies can be difficult to negotiate because they are often tied to salary bands. Negotiate your title along with your job responsibilities in order to get a higher salary. If they don't budge, request a six-month review to see if your performance warrants an increase.
Bonus	Bonuses are often tied to base salary, although there may be some wiggle room here. It is usually best to negotiate base salary.
Vacation	Larger companies usually have a set vacation policy so it may be difficult to negotiate more time.
Benefits	Benefits programs are also usually set, but you will have some flexibility on what plans you choose, which may impact your take-home pay.

If you are only asking for a small bump up in salary you could send them a note like this:

Dear Hank,

I am really looking forward to joining your team. Thank you very much for the opportunity. I have reviewed the offer and I am comfortable with everything, except the salary was lower than I had hoped. I'm willing to accept the offer as-is because I'm excited about working for Osinsure, but if you could approve an additional $5,000 per year in salary or bonus I would really appreciate it. Please let me know.

Sincerely

Sally Smith

A note like this sets a cooperative tone and lets the hiring manager know that you aren't trying to play hardball. A note like this can work like magic!

Don't worry too much about negotiating every penny and benefit from early jobs in your career. As you get more experience and become more accomplished, you will have more leverage and more options. For now, take a job that will pay you enough to cover your bills and provide some spending money. Your real value will be the experience you gain and the opportunities for growth.

Day One

Congratulations! You now have a job in the insurance industry. Now you actually have to start earning your salary and making a positive contribution. Always keep this in mind: no matter where you work, you are being paid to add value to the company. The more value you can add to the company, the more you will be worth and the more you will get paid. The less value you bring to the company, the more likely you are to lose your job.

It's always good to show up early for work. If everyone shows up at 9:00 and you show up at 8:00, you will have an extra hour per day of uninterrupted work time. This will add an additional 250 hours of working time per year which is like getting an extra month of work—think how far ahead you can get with all that time! However, on your first day of work, don't show up an hour early. Be prompt. If you show up early on your first day, someone will have to look after you until the day gets rolling!

The first day of work is usually pretty structured. In most cases you will meet the other people in your department, get settled in your desk, and fill out a bunch of paperwork for the HR department. You will probably need to have a few things with you that you don't normally carry around—like your Social

Security card, passport and birth certificate. Some companies will have formal training programs that you will go through with other new employees. These may or may not commence on your first day of work.

After the housekeeping tasks, you will probably be in meetings most of the day with coworkers. On the first day you should keep your ears open far more than your mouth. Learn as much as you can and take notes. Ask questions—a lot of them. Now is the time to ask the simple questions that may make you look dumb later on. I once worked for a company that did travel marketing. They kept talking about "Y" fare and I had no idea what it meant. I waited several months before I had the nerve to ask. By then I should have known better and I was criticized for not knowing by some of the senior team. ("Y" fare is defined as the full, not-discounted airfare.) Don't make this mistake; ask as many questions as you want.

If you are a recent college grad with little or no real work experience, you have the advantage of a fresh perspective and you may have a lot of good ideas. However, if you blurt out too many ideas or make definitive statements, you run the risk of coming across as arrogant. People with more experience may criticize you for being naive or inexperienced. Until you prove your value to the firm, you will need to find a way to communicate in a non-threatening way. One way to do this is to imply your "ownership" of your statements. For instance, let's say you are in a meeting where they are reviewing direct mail copywriting. You don't think one of the headlines is effective. You might be tempted to say:

> *This headline doesn't really connect well with the consumer. People want peace of mind when buying insurance and this headline is frightening. It's better to make people feel safe than nervous.*

This may be a good point, but the people who have been working on this campaign may feel defensive about your statement. They clearly know more than you about this program, and who are you to start making statements like this about their work? A better way to say it would be this:

> In my experience, *people want peace of mind when buying insurance.* I feel that *this headline is frightening and* may not *connect well with the consumer.* I think it's always nicer *to make people feel safe than nervous.*

In this second example the same message comes across, but it is received as your personal opinion and shows your sensitivity to others. Being mindful of how you communicate early on will help you establish good working relationships with your managers and peers.

First Few Weeks

During the first few weeks on the job you will want to make sure you live up to the expectations you set during the interview process. This will be on everyone's mind, so if you fall short of what you promised, you will let people down. Look back at your interview notes to make sure you are touching on people's hot-buttons and delivering the value you said you could.

You will want to make sure you set up a regular time with your manager to review your work and clarify assignments. Always be prepared for these meetings and never, ever cancel them. Even if you are sick at home you can still do a phone call with your manager. Being clear about expectations and demonstrating your productivity are essential elements for success.

It's also important to secure some "early wins." An early win is some kind of significant accomplishment in which you played a key role. If you are in sales, for instance, work extra hard to bring in a few new clients as soon as you can. You will want to keep people feeling good about hiring you and build some momentum. This means you will have to prioritize your work in a way that allows you to capture some of this short-term success. You can discuss these kinds of things with your manager when you meet with him or her.

On an ongoing basis you should keep notes on your accomplishments and failures. Keeping a log or dairy will not only help you learn how to do a better job in the future, but also will help you negotiate your advancement in the company over time. Being able to show a track record of accomplishments will come in handy. Don't hog the spotlight, and be sure to give credit when credit is due, but keep tabs on your own performance.

Long Term

Over the long term you will have all sorts of opportunities for growth and learning. As mentioned before, insurance companies are places of endless possibilities. Your success will depend on what kind of employee you are. This book isn't a comprehensive guide for your career, but hopefully plants a seed to help you think about your future.

It is quite common for managers to think about their employees as A, B, or C employees. Some companies even treat these as formal designations. In general, A performers are rare. They tend to get the promotions, the raises, and the accolades. B performers are more common. They are the foundation of any good company but tend to stay in one job for most of their careers. C performers are moved out of the company. In many cases C performers are simply in the wrong job, but in other cases they aren't very disciplined people.

When considering what kind of employee you will be, it is helpful to know the difference between A, B, and C performers.

A performers take the company forward in a meaningful way. Goals are benchmarks, not the end game. They put the needs of the overall business first with an understanding that personal rewards follow corporate gains. They bolster team spirit through optimism, energy, creativity, and respect.

B performers tend to maintain the status quo, serve the business well, and strive to meet, but not exceed goals. Their focus is on personal compensation, but they are happy when the company succeeds.

C performers have a negative impact on the overall growth and expansion of the team's efforts. They bring negativity and skepticism to the process and actively build walls around them in an attempt to protect their jobs, knowing their jobs may be in jeopardy. They blame others for failure and lack of advancement.

Insurance companies don't have a lot of room for C performers and they don't last long. B performers are an important part of running the company and many B performers are happy working at insurance companies, and the insurance companies are happy to have them. They get their work done well and on time, but they don't care about getting ahead.

Insurance companies, like most companies, love A performers. Insurance companies have the ability to reward A performers with promotions, bonuses, raises, and other incentives, because insurance companies grow when A performers are working there.

If you want to be an A performer at an insurance company, you will have a rich and rewarding career! You have to decide what kind of employee you will be—nobody will decide it for you. Throughout your life you will make decisions about your career and the role it plays in your overall happiness. There will always be tradeoffs between work, family, recreation, and other aspects of your life. It's your choice; choose what will make you happiest.

Chapter Nine:

CONCLUSION

Insurance is a noble profession. It has been around for many years and will be around for many more. It protects people from hardships and events outside of their control and helps them stay on track for achieving their dreams.

Without insurance, people would take fewer risks and accomplish less in life. Many good people would be forced into unbearable financial ruin in spite of their best efforts. The world would not be as happy without insurance companies.

If you are someone with an interest in becoming part of this industry, the information in this book will give you enough to get started, but it's only a small step in the right direction. Hopefully, you will be able to apply the knowledge in this book to your own success and find yourself a place in insurance.

No matter what you plan to do in life, your extra understanding of the insurance industry will be helpful. Everyone needs insurance sooner or later—and so will you!

We hope you have good luck and never bad luck!

ABOUT THE AUTHORS

Mike Moyer has spent his career writing, teaching and working in business. His experience includes a wide variety of industries including insurance industry clients, education, technology, consumer goods and even fine wine.

Mike has a MS in Integrated Marketing Communication from Northwestern University and an MBA from the University of Chicago. He teaches business and management at both universities covering topics ranging from marketing, sales, finance, operations and career strategy.

Mike is also the author of *How to Make Colleges Want You*, *Slicing Pie*, *Pitch Ninja*, *Trade Show Samurai* and *Perfect Parent Hats*.

Jerry Fuller is the Executive Director of the James S. Kemper Foundation an organization dedicated to developing well-rounded future business leaders with a special focus on the insurance industry.

Prior to joining the Kemper Foundation, Jerry was the Executive Director of the Associated Colleges of Illinois (ACI), a network of four year, non-profit, private colleges and universities. Under Jerry's leadership, the ACI became one of the most successful higher education associations in the nation, winning an unprecedented four Distinguished Performance Awards from the Foundation for Independent Higher Education, the George W. Foreman Innovation Award, and Awards of Excellence from the Workforce Board of Metropolitan Chicago and the National College Access Network.

Jerry is a graduate of Northwestern University, received his MBA from The University of Chicago, and completed the Strategic Perspectives in Nonprofit Management Program at the Harvard Business School.

Insurance Basics Online Course

The online Insurance Basics course is available at **www.JSKemper.org**.